MW00651367

Five Stops

by Carolyn Kelly

illustrated by Jaime Smith

Phonics Skill: Consonant *Gg/g/*
High-Frequency Words: *one, two, three, four, five*

PEARSON

Scott
Foresman

I am Sam.

I stop at five stops
with my big bus.

Nat and Nan hop on
at stop one.
Lin skips on with Nat and Nan.

At stop two, Gil and Gab
hop on the big bus.
Dad and little Sal can not.

I stop for Ann and Dan.

They hop on at stop three.

Kim skips on at stop four.

Not Tim. He has lots of dots.

The last one on is Kip.

He got on at stop five.

He sits with Lin.

I drop the kids at the flag.
Nat, Nan, Lin, Gil, Gab, Ann,
Dan, Kim, and Kip hop and skip.